Islamic geometric patterns for coloring:

Activity book to color and enjoy a relaxing day.

Marisol Paredes

Introduction

Mandalas have fascinated people throughout the centuries and for good reason. It relieves you of stress and helps you to be more relaxed, you can color it in the company of your relatives.

At Marisol Paredes Publications we have decided to compile coloring pages of these mandalas for your coloring pleasure.

We hope you enjoy them fully!

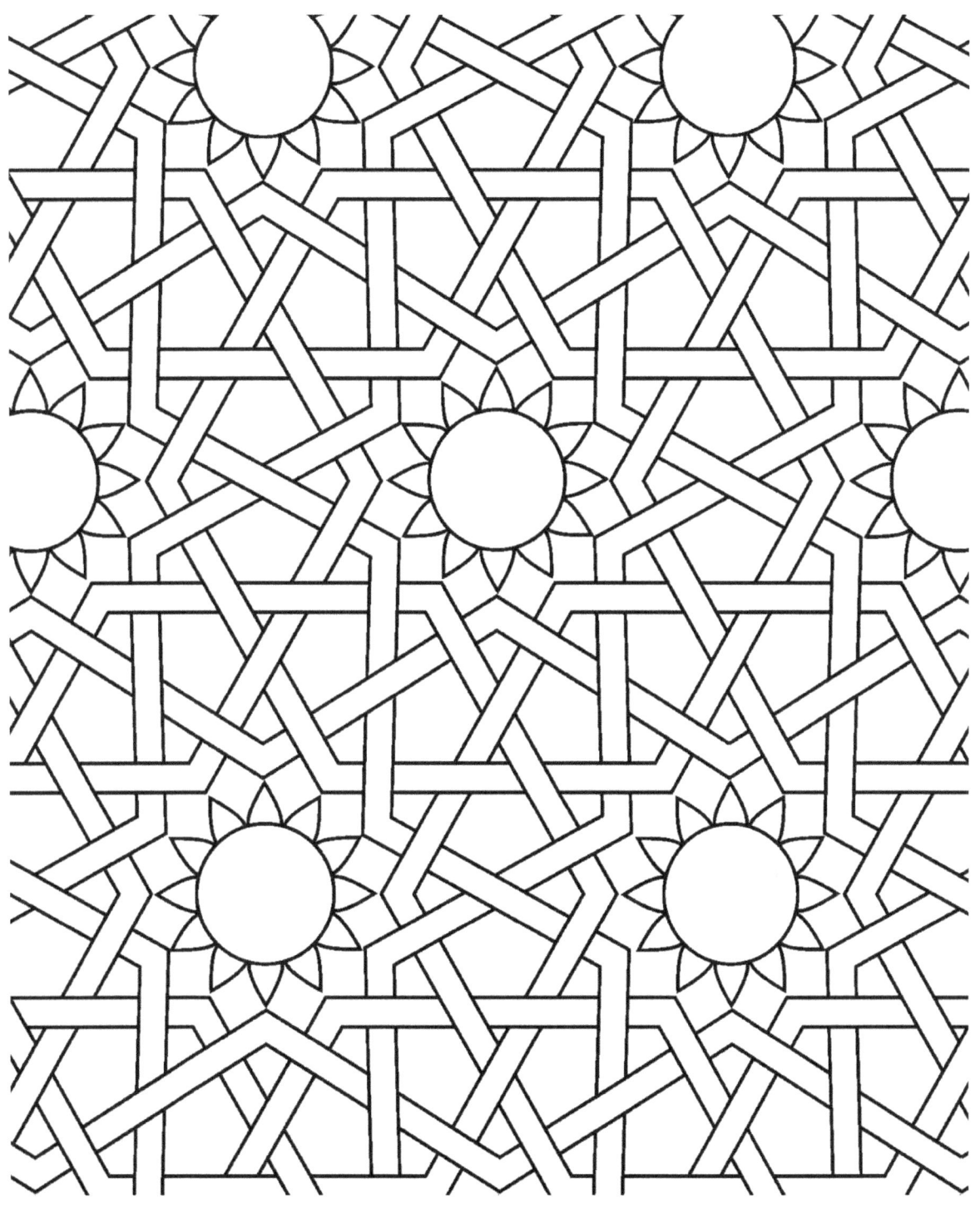

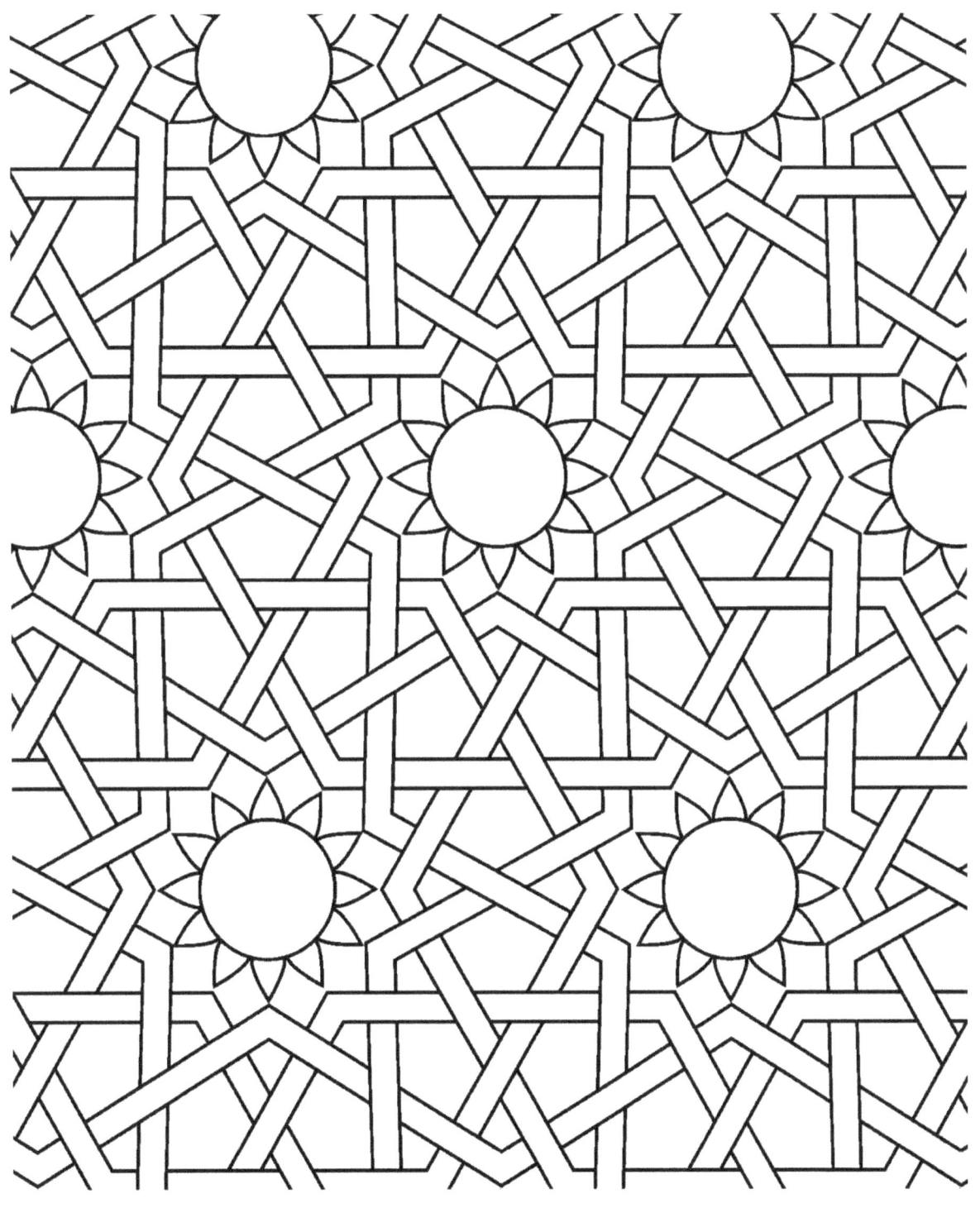

8

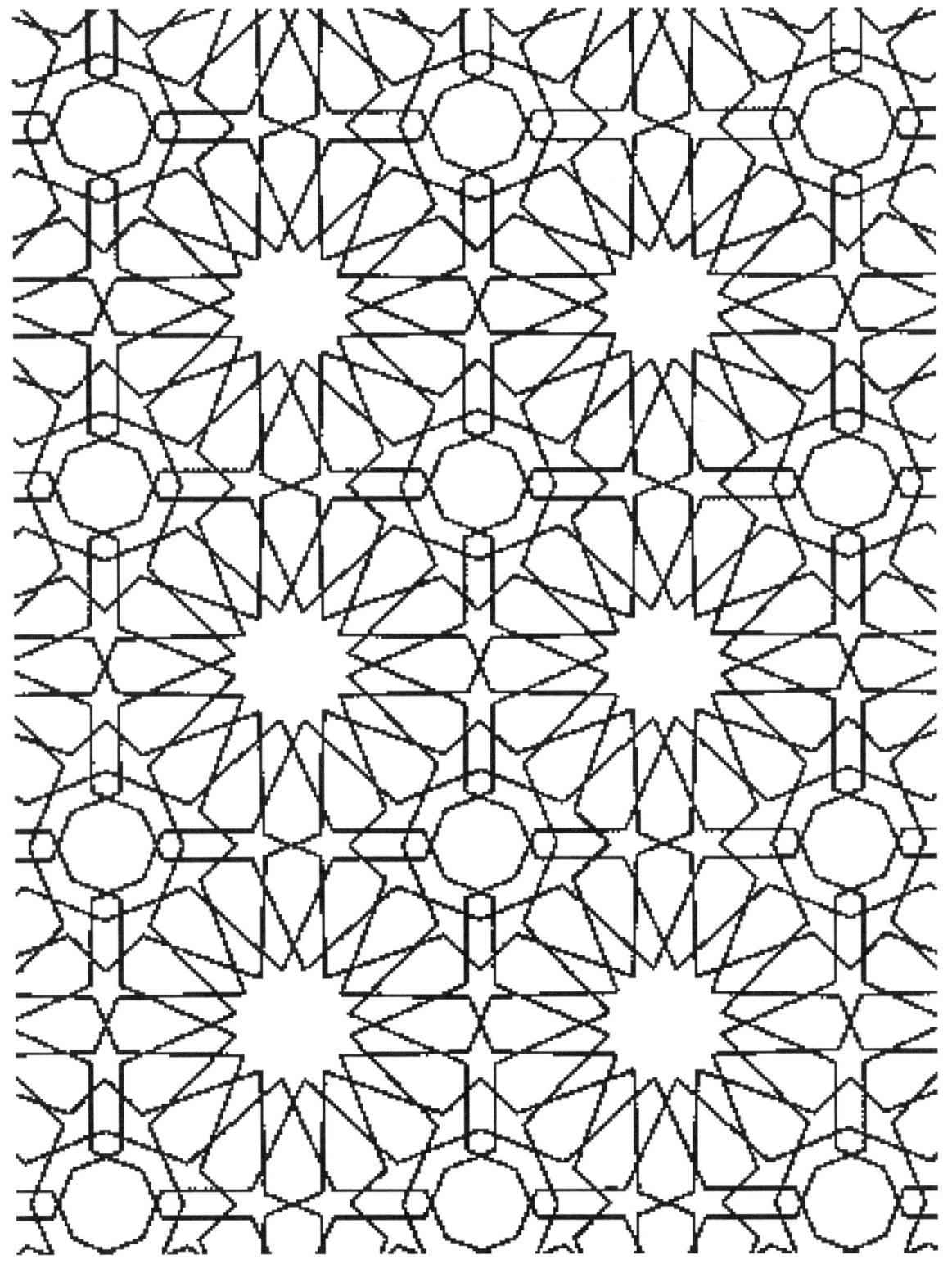

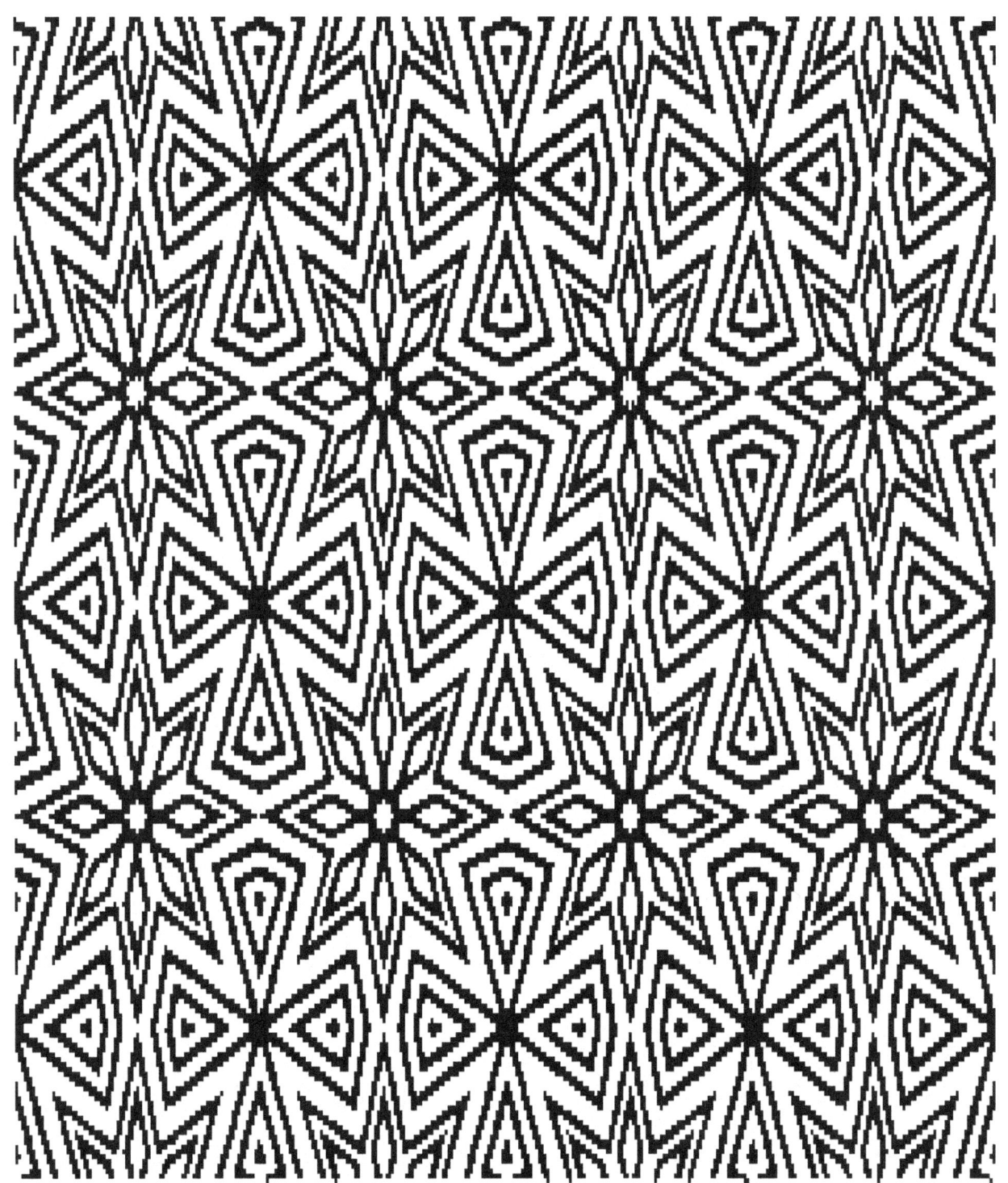

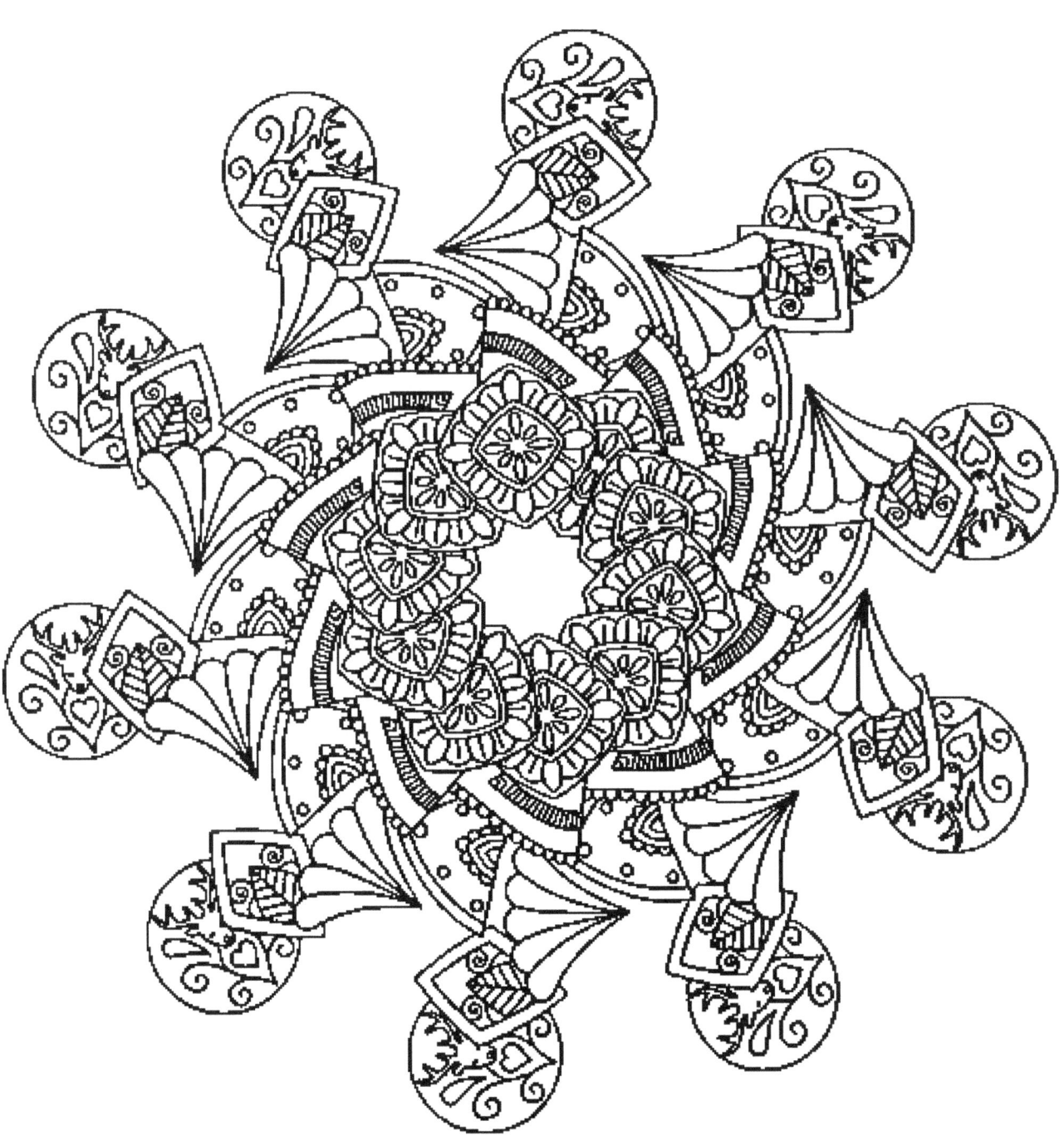

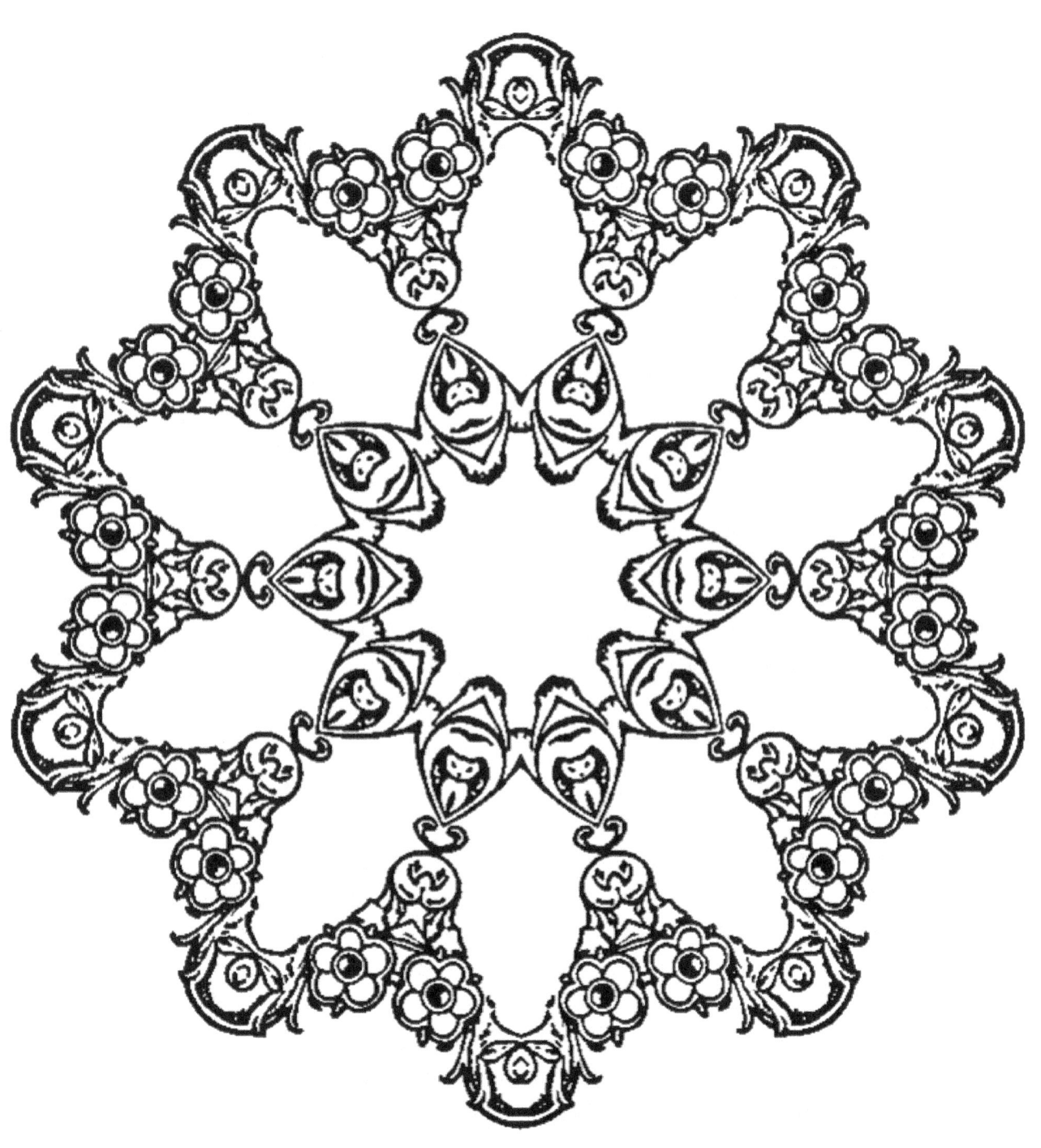

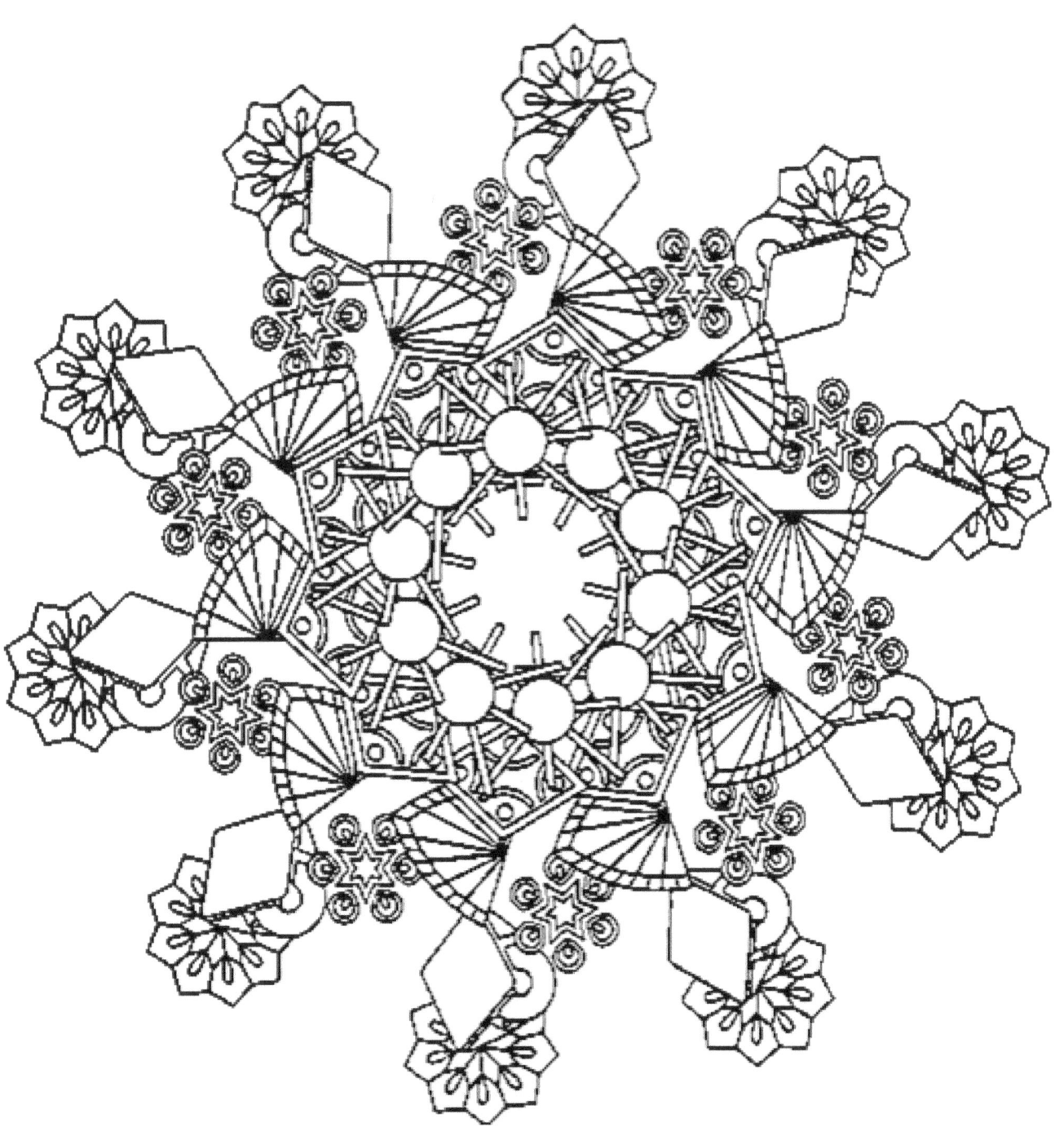

17

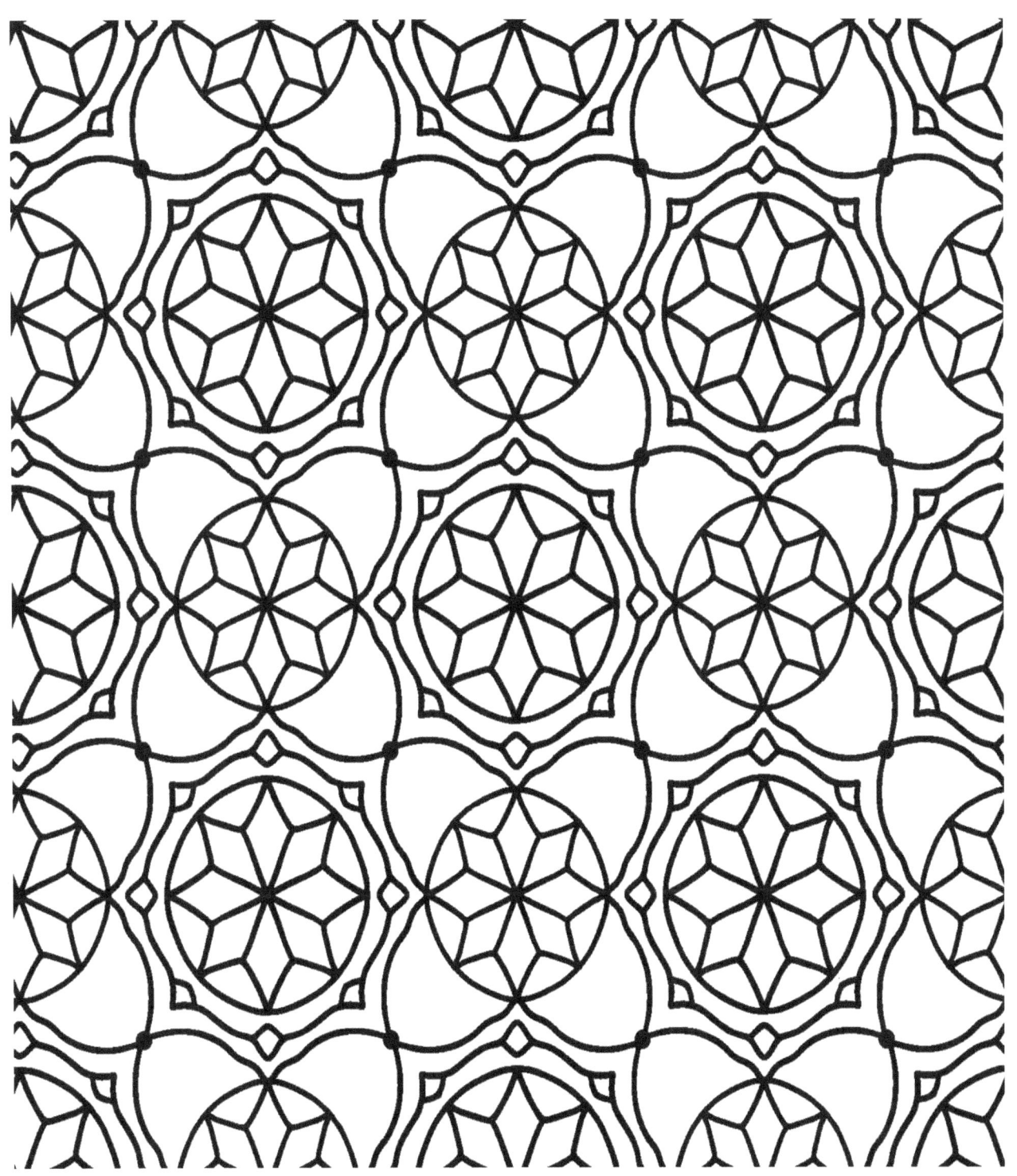

19

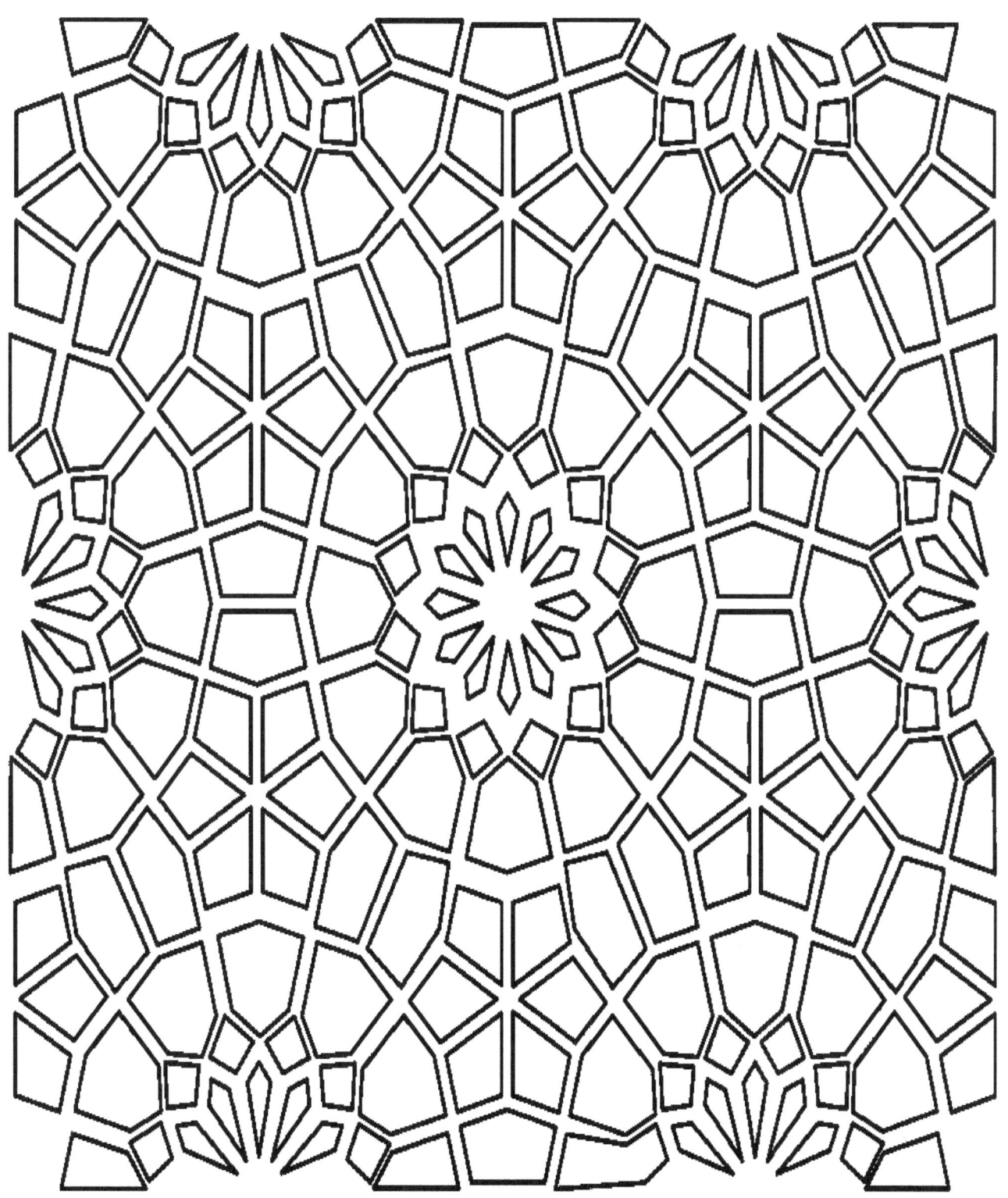

21

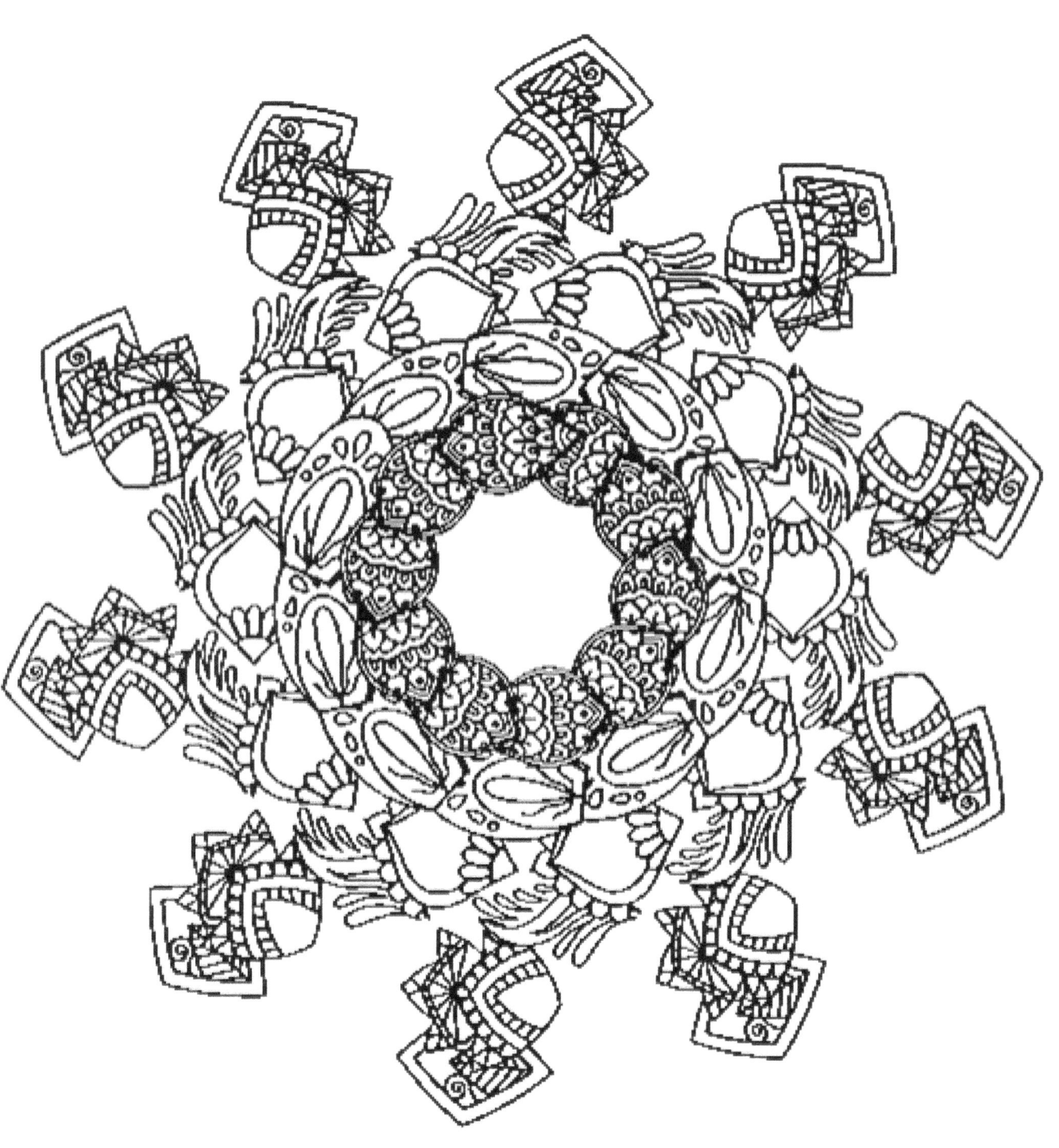

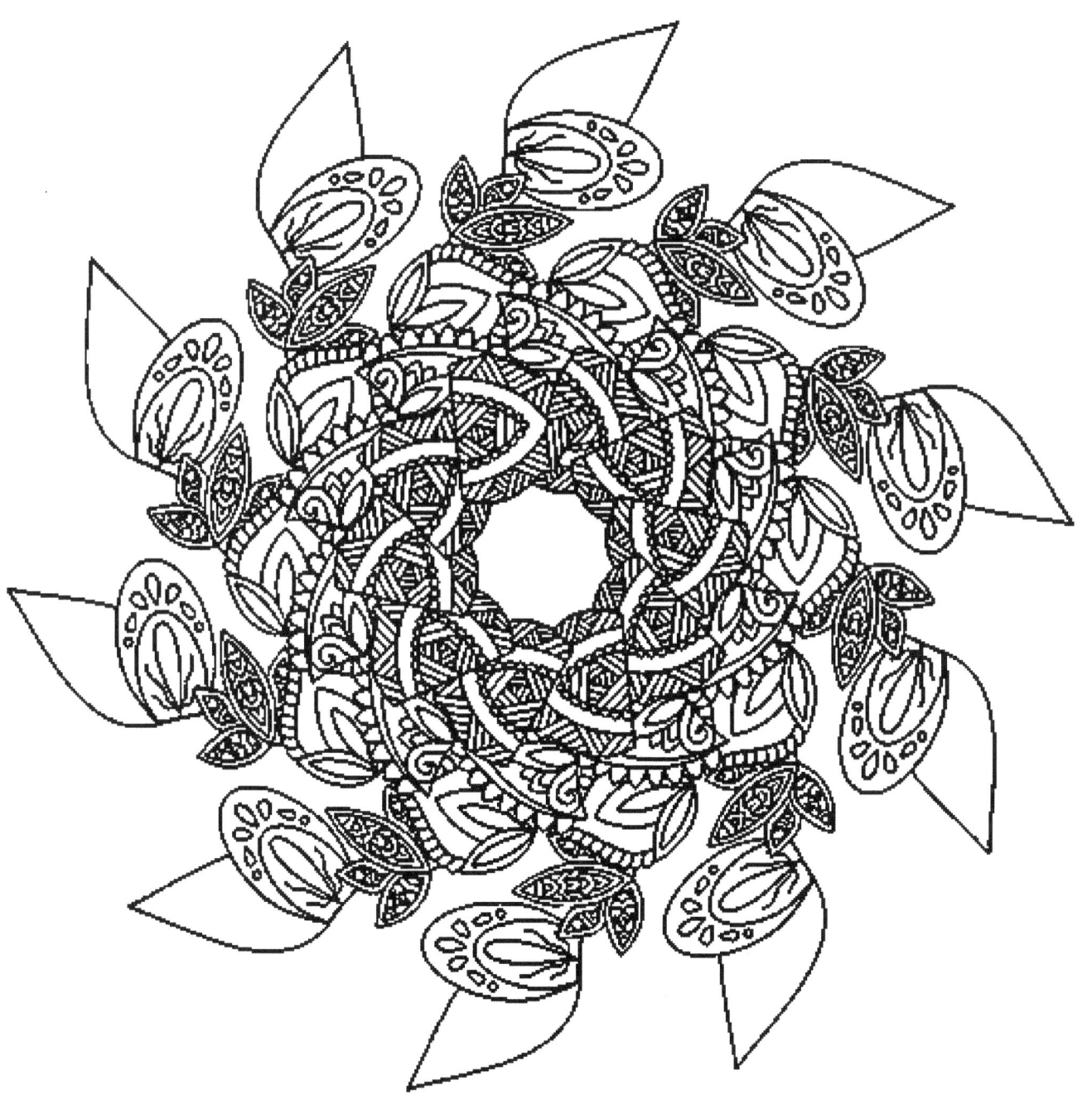

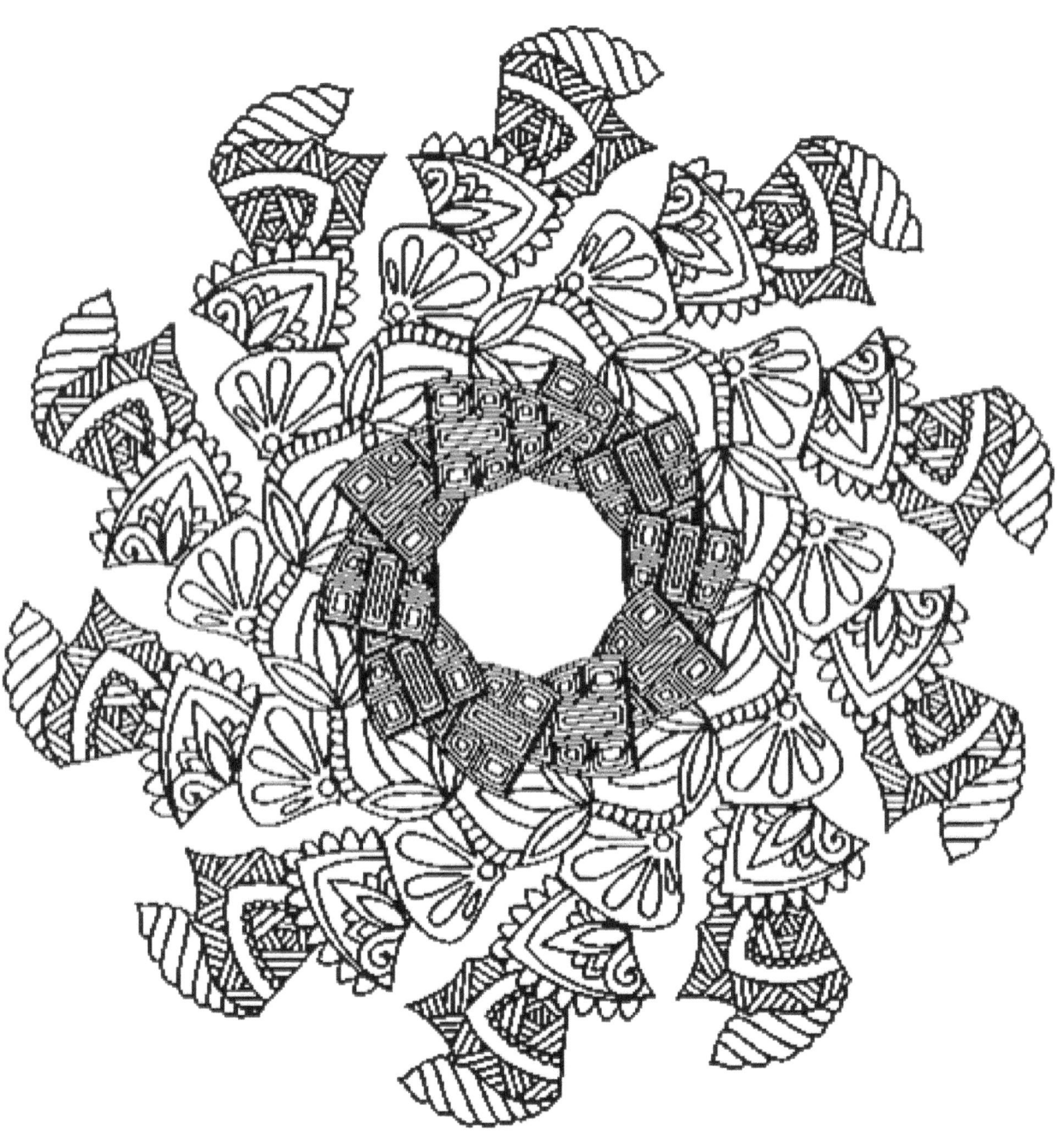

Conclusion

Thank you so much for purchasing this book. If you enjoyed it, then please leave an Amazon review. Reviews are the lifeblood of our publishing endeavors- leaving a positive review would mean the world to us.

Cheers!

- Marisol Paredes